Collins

FOUNDATION LEVEL 3

LITTLE LEARNERS

RHYMES AND STORIES

SERIES EDITOR: RANI T.

Published by Collins Learning
A division of HarperCollins*Publishers*
India Private Limited

HarperCollins Publishers
Building No 10, Tower A, 4th Floor,
DLF Cyber City, Phase II, Gurgaon 122002

1 London Bridge Street, London, SE1 9GF,
United Kingdom

2 Bloor Street East, Toronto, Ontario M4W
1A8, Canada

Lvl 13, 201 Elizabeth Street (PO Box A565,
NSW, 1235), Sydney NSW 2000, Australia

195 Broadway, New York, NY 10007, USA

Browse the complete Collins catalogue at
www.collins.in
For any queries/feedback, please write to us
at **SCHOOLSUPPORT@harpercollins.co.in** or
call us on 0124-4894800.

First published in 2020

Reprint: 10 9 8 7 6 5 4 3 2 1

ISBN: 978-93-5357-047-7

Artwork and layout by
Qualibre Creatives Pvt. Ltd.

Printed and bound by
MicroPrints India, New Delhi

Acknowledgements

Cover: HarperCollins*Publishers*India

Title Page: HarperCollins*Publishers*India

Prelim Pages: radenmas, denkcreative, nonohana, graphic-bee

Inside: Pg 23: Teguh Mujiono, GraphicsRF, Tigatelu, kompozit; **pg 24:** MerggyR, volkanakmese, Teguh Mujiono; **pg 25:** Volkanakmese, Naddya, GraphicsRF, Vestery; **pg 26:** MerggyR, volkanakmese, Teguh Mujiono; **pg 27:** Volkanakmese, Naddya, GraphicsRF, Vestery; **pg 28:** Pink Leon, exxorian, nyamol, ONYXprj; **pg 29:** artisticco, bennyb, exxorian; **pg 30:** MerggyR, volkanakmese, Teguh Mujiono; **pg 31:** Teguh Mujiono, Exxorian; **pg 32:** Naddya, Teguh Mujiono, Tigatelu; **pg 33:** Teguh Mujiono, GraphicsRF, Tigatelu, kompozit, chihhang; **pg 34:** aleksey-martynyuk, Akindo, Naddiya; **pg 35:** aleksey-martynyuk, Akindo, Naddiya; **pg 36:** aleksey-martynyuk, Akindo, Naddiya;

Preface

Collins Little Learners, comprising 20 books in all, provides graded, age-appropriate learning opportunities targeting holistic skill development for children in the age group of 3 years to 6 years. Spread across three levels, the series spans **English**, **Maths**, **General Awareness**, **Art and Craft** and **Hindi**. The series comes bundled with a **workbook** for English and a book of **rhymes and stories** for each level. The books use a combination of hands-on activities, frequent recapitulation and child-friendly artwork to facilitate learning.

The early years are the most significant years for growth, development and learning. During this period, children need adequate opportunities for stimulating experiences as these favourably affect various learning abilities. Learning experiences, when chosen and planned properly, fuel the innate curiosity of children, and stimulate their thought processes.

Learning and Development During the Early Years

The goal of learning during the early years is to enhance the all-round development of personality and to inculcate healthy attitudes, life skills and good values. Creative play, well thought-out games and developmentally appropriate activities help children develop the necessary skills to achieve these goals. The skills that children need to acquire can broadly be categorized as:

Motor: Motor skills pertain not only to gross motor activities like walking and jumping but also include fine motor activities like the ability to hold a pencil and write. The development of motor skills is facilitated through several graded activities.

Personal, Social and Emotional: Personal, social and emotional development, necessary for the overall personality development of children, is achieved using a combination of hands-on activities, role plays and thought-provoking stories and rhymes.

Linguistic: The ability to listen, speak, read and write is critical to success in formal learning environments.

Mathematical: The development of mathematical ideas and concepts is important at this stage since children will continue to build on this learning for most of their years of schooling.

Knowledge and Understanding of the World: This is achieved through activities that enable children to explore their surroundings at home and in the school, and interact with the people that they see around them.

Health and Safety: The idea of health and safety is introduced through activities, stories and retelling of real-life experiences to encourage children to focus on health and well-being.

Creative: Creative skills are developed through a host of activities involving art, craft, painting, roleplays, etc.

Logical and Rational Thinking: Activities that involve simple puzzles, pattern-completion and visual discrimination help children develop logical and rational thinking skills.

The Collins Little Learners Teacher Support Materials

The series includes extensive teacher support in the form of:

Teacher's Resource Books: Comprises stories, activity banks, classroom management and assessment guidelines

Multimedia eBook: Consists of animations, audio, video, slide shows and interactive exercises

Print-ready Worksheets: Additional worksheets for practice and reinforcement, present in the digital support

Digital Flashcards: Flashcards with embedded sounds and animations for letter formation and letter-sound association

Animations and Songs: Animated stories and rhymes set to tune

Interactive Games: Interactivities to reinforce concepts in a fun and engaging manner

A note on the activity banks (included in the Teacher's Manuals)

The activity banks comprise hands-on activities that will help children develop the requisite skills to attain age-appropriate learning goals. In keeping with Howard Gardener's theory of multiple intelligences, the activity banks include options and variations that enable teachers to provide a planned cycle of experiences and opportunities, which foster each type of intelligence, to every child in their classrooms. The activity banks equip teachers to use the strengths of children as a means of complementing their less developed areas by valuing and nurturing the inherent abilities of the children.

Contents

Hey Diddle Diddle

Hey diddle diddle,
The cat and the fiddle,
The cow jumped over the moon.
The little dog laughed,
To see such a sight,
And the dish ran away with the spoon.

Three Little Kittens

The three little kittens,
They lost their mittens,
And they began to cry.
"Oh, mother dear, we sadly fear
Our mittens we have lost."
"What? Lost your mittens,
You naughty kittens!
Then you shall have no pie."
"Mee-ow, mee-ow, mee-ow.
We shall have no pie.
Our mittens we have lost."
The three little kittens, they found
their mittens,
And they began to smile.
"Oh, mother dear, see here, see here,
Our mittens we have found."
"What? Found your mittens, you good little
kittens,
And you shall have some pie."
"Mee-ow, mee-ow, mee-ow.
We shall have some pie.
Let us have some pie."

A-Tisket, A-Tasket

A-tisket, a-tasket,
A green and yellow basket.
I wrote a letter to my friend
And on the way, I dropped it,
I dropped it, I dropped it,
And on the way, I dropped it.
A little boy, he picked it up
And put it in his pocket.

Goosey Goosey Gander

Goosey goosey gander,
Whither shall I wander?
Upstairs and downstairs,
And in my lady's chamber.
There I met an old man,
Who wouldn't say his prayers.
So I took him by his left leg,
And threw him down the stairs.

Little Boy Blue

Little boy blue,
Come blow your horn,
The sheep's in the meadow,
The cow's in the corn;
But where is the boy
Who looks after the sheep?
He's under a haystack,
He's fast asleep.
Will you wake him?
No, not I,
For if I do,
He's sure to cry.

Itsy Bitsy Spider

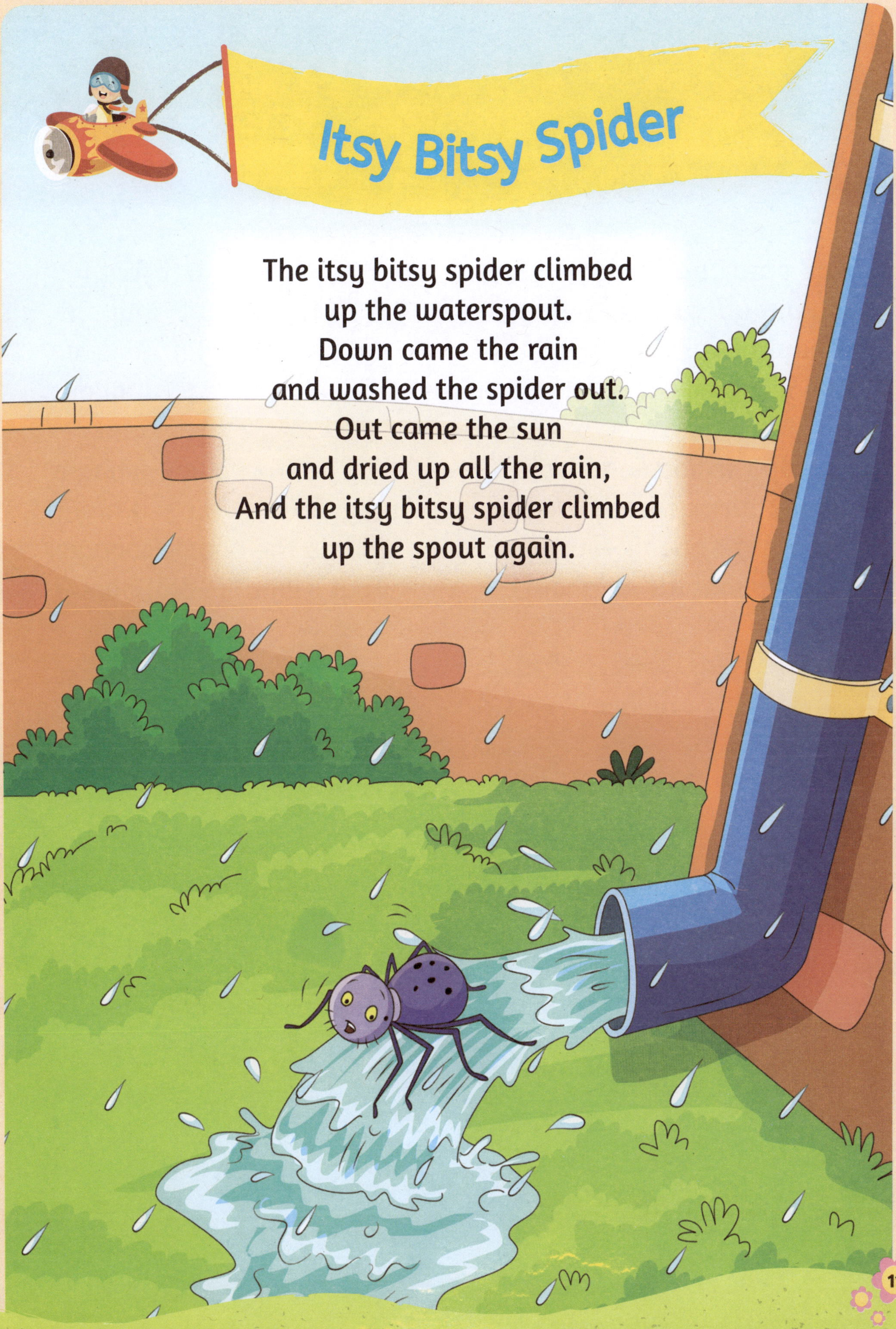

The itsy bitsy spider climbed
up the waterspout.
Down came the rain
and washed the spider out.
Out came the sun
and dried up all the rain,
And the itsy bitsy spider climbed
up the spout again.

Boogie-Woogie

You put your right foot in,
You put your right foot out;
You put your right foot in,
And you shake it all about.

You do the boogie-woogie,
And you turn yourself around.
You do the boogie-woogie,
That's what it's all about!

You put your left foot in,
You put your left foot out;
You put your left foot in,
And you shake it all about.

You do the boogie-woogie,
And you turn yourself around.
You do the boogie-woogie,
That's what it's all about!

Clean Hands

Wash, wash, wash your hands,
Wash those germs away.
Soap and water does the trick,
To keep them clean all day.

Good Manners

Hearts, like doors,
Will open with ease.
To very, very little keys.
And don't forget that two of these
Are 'I thank you',
And 'If you please'.

Brush Your Teeth

Brush your teeth, brush your teeth,
Give them all a treat.
Brush up and down and all around,
To keep them clean and neat.

In the morning and at night,
Clean them twice a day.
Brush up and down and all around,
Keep fillings well away.

Safety First

Up the street, I look to see,
If any traffic's near me.
Down the road, I look as well,
And listen for a horn or bell.

There's something, coming–wait a bit,
If I run out, I may be hit.
But now the road is really clear,
No cars or motor bus is near.
I'll run across the road so wide,
And get safety on the other side.

The Postman

Here comes the postman,
With a sack on his back.
He's coming up the path,
With a rat-a-tat-a-tat.

I wonder what he's brought,
Quick, let's see.
A letter for Daddy,
Oh! And one for me.

Hickory Dickory Dock

Hickory Dickory Dock,
The mouse ran up the clock.
The clock struck one,
The mouse ran down!
Hickory Dickory Dock.

Hickory Dickory Dock,
The bird looked at the clock.
The clock struck two,
Away she flew!
Hickory Dickory Dock.

Hickory Dickory Dock,
The dog barked at the clock.
The clock struck three,
Fiddle-de-dee!
Hickory Dickory Dock.

Hickory Dickory Dock,
The bear slept by the clock.
The clock struck four,
He ran out the door!
Hickory Dickory Dock.

Five Little Fish

Five little fish, swimming in a pool.
The first one says, 'The pool is cool,'
The second one says, 'The pool is deep,'
The third one says, 'I want to sleep',
The fourth one says, 'Let's dive and dip,
The fifth one says, 'I see a ship'.

A fisherman's boat comes,
The line goes splash.
The five little fish,
Swim away in a flash.

One Little Bee

One little bee flew and flew,
He met a friend and that made two.
Two little bees, busy as could be,
Along came another and that made three.
Three little bees, wanted one more,
Found one soon and that made four.
Four little bees, going to the hive.
Found their little brother,
And that made five.

The Wheels on the Bus

The wheels on the bus go round and round,
Round and round,
Round and round.
The wheels on the bus go round and round,
all day long.

The horn on the bus goes beep, beep, beep,
Beep, beep, beep,
Beep, beep, beep.
The horn on the bus goes beep, beep, beep,
all day long.

The wipers on the bus go swish, swish, swish,
Swish, swish, swish,
Swish, swish, swish.
The wipers on the bus go swish, swish, swish,
all day long.

If You're Happy and You Know It

If you're happy and you know it, clap your hands!
If you're happy and you know it, clap your hands!
If you're happy and you know it, and you really want to show it,
If you're happy and you know it, clap your hands!

(Repeat with "stomp your feet", "shout Hurray!", "do all three".)

The Ant and the Grasshopper

This is a story about two friends– Annie Ant and Gabby Grasshopper. Annie worked very hard in summer. She stored food for the winter. She did not waste any time. Gabby danced in summertime and played with the flowers and the birds.

Soon, the summer sun faded and winter came. The flowers dried up. The birds flew away. Everything was covered in snow. Gabby was shivering in the cold. He tried to wrap a leaf around himself to keep warm. All his friends were gone. He did not have any food to eat. He was hungry and tired.

Annie ant sat in front of a fire. She was warm.
She had food for winter.
She was happy.

Gabby walked on and on, looking for food. After some time, he saw a yellow light. Gabby knocked on the door. Annie opened the door. Gabby said, "Hello, Annie! Can I stay with you? I am cold and hungry. I will play the fiddle for you. You will not get bored."

Annie was sad to see Gabby. She said, “How thin you have become! You played your fiddle all summer long. You did not prepare for winter. Now you have no food to eat. But, you are my friend. I will help you.”

Gabby said, “Thank you, Annie! You are my best friend!”

Tilly's Garden

Tilly lives in a house with a big garden. There are many plants and flowers in the garden. Tilly loves to play in the garden.

One day, a bee stung Tilly's hand. Her hand turned red. She was in a lot of pain. That night Tilly said a special prayer to take away all the bees and insects from the garden.

Next morning, there were no bees and insects in the garden.
Tilly was very happy.
She sat under the tree.
She played with the flowers.

But, something strange was happening.
Every day, the flowers seemed to become sad. Soon, they started falling off. Tilly was sad to see this.

Tilly's mother said, "Bees and insects are friends of flowers.
But there are no bees and insects in our garden. That is why the flowers are sad."
That night, Tilly said a special prayer to bring back all the bees and insects into the garden.

Next morning, the flowers and bees were playing together. Tilly was happy to see her garden blooming.

The Tale of Two Brothers

Raja and Raki are scared of lightning and thunder. Whenever they hear thunder, they run inside and hide. One day, there was loud thunder and lightning. Both boys ran to hide behind Granny.

Granny said, “Why are you so scared? Let me tell you the story of thunder and lightning. Come, sit with me!” Granny started the story. “Thunder and Lightning are two brothers, just like you. They live in the sky. Thunder talks very loudly. Lightning cannot talk. Lightning can only be seen. Both brothers love to play. But they are very scared of Mr Sun. So, the brothers can play only when the clouds come. When they play, we can hear the rumbling of thunder and see lightning! So, don’t fear thunder and lightning. Let them play and have fun.”

After listening to the story, Raja and Raki clapped their hands. They said, "Thunder and Lightning are just like us! But they are very loud. Now we are not scared anymore."
Granny kissed both and said, "You are brave boys!"